The Life of a Loner

Leonard McKey

authorHOUSE®

AuthorHouse™
1663 Liberty Drive, Suite 200
Bloomington, IN 47403
www.authorhouse.com
Phone: 1-800-839-8640

First published by AuthorHouse 12/12/2007

ISBN: 978-1-4343-4132-7 (sc)

Printed in the United States of America
Bloomington, Indiana

This book is printed on acid-free paper.

My full name is Leonard Duane McKey and even though it isn't a (BFD) big fucking deal to most people I have had my middle name spelled so many different ways it's not even funny that is why I prefer Leonard McKey and I am damn proud of my last name McKey which some people still spell it Mackey but most people pronounce it Mickey which I correct them I was born on November 21,1956 and raised in La Porte, TX I don't go out much except maybe to go eat every once in a while or to pick something up and come back to my apartment to eat to where it is quite to eat and write my books for many years I worked for my Parents but since both died years ago I just sit and write I know most People would ask how I survive my Parents set up a separate trust fund for me and my two older Sisters one I talk with every once in a while but one I never talk to which is ok with me anyway and I had many acquaintances for many years but now I have very few of course I don't want anybody feeling sorry for me or their pity besides I live a happy life lonely but happy just the same and I would rather be alone than to have either a partner or an acquaintance constantly bitching about something I had this one acquaintance that would always come to the Restaurant where I was about the same time every day asking me the same question you going to eat today and I would say yes what would you like trying to be nice to him but it became a daily ritual and he would always talk loud where everyone could hear every word and he was constantly asking me for cigarettes and/or money until finally I had enough of his filthy mouth always talking about doing this or that to the school aged waitresses working there although I was the type that never wanted to hurt anyone's feelings however I realized that nobody really gave a fuck about my feelings plus I was/am tired of being a doormat letting people walk all over me in a manner of speaking my Parents were very protective over me since I was hit by a Truck at six ½ years old in the hospital eight months and nine days as my Parents brought me home they realized the leg and foot brace which the hospital had put on my Right foot had already damaged my right foot and after many trip to and from the hospital getting therapy my Parents started giving me the therapy at home I can't actually remember when I started back to school but I did graduate in 1975 most of time was spent with the program on the job training some years later I got married to a Woman that I had clean my house she was a live-in House-keeper which I found out after we were married that she was already married with five Daughters but it didn't last even a year and got annulled or so I thought which was a divorce instead after some time passed a Minister that attended the Church which I attended many years ago told me about a young Woman that did attend the Church but her and her Parents and Sisters and Brother had moved and that she was very lonely also and after a little time I went up to visit her and her Family she and I went to a few different places alone without her Son on her skirt I can't remember how long I was there but I remember that she and I had sex in the back seat of the Van I had at that time, as I got back to my House in La Porte after a little time had passed she called me and said that she was pregnant which was a lie but I didn't find out until after I drove back up and proposed to her where I had to get down on one knee and ask her Dad if I could marry her he said yes so I moved her and her Son down to La Porte to my House and that is when the problems began I work for my Parents Construction Company but when I came Home from work she said go take a shower to where we can eat not giving me any time to even catch my breath or anything, I thought she was just pulling my chain but she continued this shit every evening as I got Home and I started going out after work drinking just to put up with her mouth and the way she was when she wanted me for anything she would say get over here now of course this was after the Minister from the Church had Married us but another thing that was something else she didn't want me to leave to even go to work she want me to stay there where we could make love she told me this over and over again and again but she would not go shopping without me either where as we got to the isle with the feminine products she would always ask if I needed anything there and she spoke loud to where others could hear and her Son acted like a little brat in the Store also and her Son wasn't mine it was from a previous affair she had, but the thing she would do that really burnt my ass was anytime we needed to talk about a problem she would always call her Mother long distance plus her Dad was a Truck driver and I had to go work on his Truck every time he was in Houston and buy the parts to fix it also but I can't remember what it was about but we had a problem and she said I'm going to call my Mother I said oh no your not as she walked into the bedroom I was behind her as she picked up the receiver I pulled the Telephone cord out of the wall but she wouldn't shut-up and I slapped her on the bed and said bitch your going Home and within time she and her Son went back then after some time passed I met a Woman working at a Restaurant where I knew the people that owned the Restaurant and they tried to warn me about that Woman but I was so lonely and horny I felt I couldn't live without her and after just a matter of months I discovered that the trips she would take every Month she claimed to see her Parents which she never wanted me to meet sounded strange from the start but I didn't push but as every trip became another day longer and another day plus I found out from my own Mother that the Woman was taking the money I made and putting in her checking account out of town to where when we divorced she would have something to fall back on and one day as I got home from work I told her that I wanted a divorce and she had the nerve to stand there and ask me why and she said you don't love me any more and I said no I don't she acted like it shocked her but the bitch knew it was coming and she had enough nerve to ask if she could stay until she found a place to live which I agreed to I got something's and slept at an office until my Dad went and told her to go and she left however she was a good fuck when we did have sex but every month as she said she was on her period she always slept in the other room I was so relieved when she left as some time past I got back involved with that young Woman that use to attend the Church I attended back then which was a mistake since she told me what to do and when to do it which didn't last very long at all which ended in divorce but before we divorced again she introduced some friends of hers which after she and I were divorced the second time introduced me to their niece which had been married before and divorced I met her Parents and her son and her niece also and I thought that she and I might have had a chance but every time she and I went out her aunt and uncle were with us every time where we had no time together without someone standing right there but it went on for some time until one day her aunt said some thing about going out of town and asked me and her niece to go also and her husband went with us as well we left one night I drove all night as we arrived at the hotel we got one room which I wasn't aware of that all of us would be sharing a room where I did not even rest any due to the fact that the Woman and her niece were sharing a bed and me and the Woman's husband was to share the other bed and there was no way in hell that I was going to share a bed with another Man so I stayed up after her husband rested some he had the nerve to come to me and say why don't you let her their niece enjoy the trip and later that evening we all four of us went to a shop right across from Elvis's house there in Memphis Tennessee where me and their niece were never together without one or both her aunt and uncle watching over every move which was very irritating but when we got back to the hotel where I got a room by myself I tried to rest but couldn't thinking about what her Uncle said after a while I thought fuck this so I went turned in my room key and left coming back home where I stopped at a rest area for a little bit and then went on home where there were messages from them but I didn't care I remember my Parents sent them money to come home which I wouldn't have done but my Parents did but as they returned the Man and his Wife came to my house at that time and all the shit I had to listen to he said that he had just gotten up and didn't know what he was saying was his excuse which was completely no excuse whatsoever since in the past as I was very young I was taught that when you don't know what your saying to keep your mouth shut which ended any chances with their niece which was doomed from the beginning my most recent relationship was with a Woman I met online after talking with her online and by phone for quite some time the Woman and her teenage daughter came down after a week I flew with them to her hometown after about a week up there they came back home with me for a couple months in that time one night her daughter was in dire pain and crying from the pain her Mother was telling me that she would be all-right but I didn't listen so me and the Woman and her daughter went to the emergency room where we found that her daughter had a female problem as we left the emergency room both her Mother and the daughter was glad that I insisted taking her daughter to the emergency room but we didn't get married I was taking more blood pressure medicine than I was supposed too that it was a sign to me that I am supposed to be alone after I sent the Woman and her daughter back to their hometown which my Dad took her and her Daughter to the Air port for me and after my Dad died, I inherited the Ranch where I lived for many years in a separate house, then as I moved into the house which my Parents had built which I lived in for years until one morning I wanted to watch television but couldn't because I thought the wind had moved the television antenna again which happened quite often, but I decided to go to sleep as I was about out I heard something but I went to sleep since there was there never any problem before at my Ranch, since I lived there which was since 1982 or 83 as I slept, I got knocked out hit over the head, as I woke up I discovered I was bleeding badly after I checked things in the other room's I called 911 were the Sheriff Department and Emergency Medical

Services responded immediately after answering many questions by the Sheriff Department I was transported to the Emergency room at the Baytown Methodist Hospital where I was told I didn't need stitches my Nephew and his Wife met me at the Hospital where they drove me over to my Sister's and Brother-in-law where my Nephew and Sister drove me back to me Ranch where I got something's together and went to a Motel where for several nights I got blood on the pillows from being hit on the head then after spending a few weeks at the Motel one morning I thought what the fuck am I doing driving 30 miles one way every day to Liberty and I called and got a Motel room in Liberty where I spent about 3- four weeks until I got into an Apartment which I really like even though I live alone I am not alone, I like helping people not with money since I am not able too but through advice about a job or personal advice through my experiences with both work or personal related questions I am the type of Man that if a person has a question about something I have experienced I will help them but if it is something that I haven't experienced I am not / will not stand there and advise a person with advice that would come back and bite me in the ass I have many years of experience in Construction and even though I haven't been married that long either time I do know what a Woman likes in or out of the bedroom I am not claiming that I know everything about Women I use to drink but I haven't had a drink in over almost 30 years I live in La Porte, TX for many years since that is where my Parents owned a Construction Business which my Dad started back in 1951 which for several years I worked at the Business doing different things from operating some equipment to mechanic work I moved to the Ranch in 1982-83 which I inherited as my Parents died which I sold but as my Parents were living in 1992 or 93 me and my Dad decided to close the Construction Business since it was not making any money since I was the Secretary-Treasurer in the Business after the Equipment was sold the Business became McKey Enterprises, Inc. Where I kept records on things since there was some Equipment at the Ranch plus I was in charge of making payroll and deposits at the Bank which I did where my Mother & Sisters and I would have money that week which continued for years until my Mother died in 1997 then the payroll was to my Sisters and I then in 2001 as my Dad became very sick I continued keeping the books until my Dad told me that I needed to sign the books over to my Sisters which I thought sounded very strange but I did and upon his death I received money to hold things over till the Trust started paying my Sisters and I monthly which was fine but after time past I found out that the Bank over the Trust was planning to auction off the Equipment at the Ranch I inherited in their Wills both my Mother and Dad which stated that I was to inherit the Ranch which I did but it also stated that I was to inherit the Cattle and the Equipment on the Ranch but the bank auctioned off both the Cattle and Equipment but unknown to the Bank I was told by my Dad to sale certain pieces of the Equipment but I couldn't the Bank had a police officer at the gate to my Ranch to prevent me from selling any Equipment which was wrong since I knew the Equipment was paid off as well as the Ranch property but the bank went through with the auction of both the Equipment there at the Ranch which I went over and watched in disbelief that this was happening right before my eyes but it was really happening after which I cried as the Equipment was moved out remembering what my Dad had told me many times that when he died he wanted me to sale certain things and keep the rest but needless to say after the auction I was left with nothing much at my Ranch since the auctioneer had come out sometime before the auction and if something was locked he would break the lock to either gain entrance or to look at the contents therein and even though I had some Cattle my self the auctioneer even wanted the money for that even though I sold some Bulls with my Cattle which I had every right to do so then the bank had the Cattle and Bulls moved to another City to auction off the Cattle but since then I had Leased most of the property out Except the front property for a while then I Leased it to another Man but finally had to break the monthly Lease between me and the person that made it tough on me since I had to hire a person to come mow the front property and the pond pasture which was I called the front 40 where the house was at that I lived in after my Dad died years before I lived in a trailer house for a while then my Parents bought a wood frame house where I lived until my Dad died then I moved over into the house he lived in which I knew he wanted me to and planned spending the rest of my life there until the morning when I was attacked in my own house as I mentioned earlier I love living here at the Apartment complex even though I don't know many people living here at the complex the people I have met are nice and polite however this is a pretty quite Apartment complex which I like to where I can think and write my books another thing is the utility bill is of course with another Company but where I was spending somewhere a pretty good amount on just electricity plus here I have garbage service where at my Ranch I was burning my garbage but the main thing is even though I live alone I'm not alone however I went back to one blood pressure pill a day as was prescribed by the Doctor I was seeing at that time since I have lived alone for most of my life I am not/will not have any Woman living with me or getting married to tell me what to do and when and how to do it that will not work since I've been there and done that I know many people would say hey get a life but not being able to work and not many friends I have always done what was asked of me but I am no damn robot that does whatever is either asked or requested of me however I must admit that a while back I did almost anything asked of me but I am not going to be a doormat any more because I have a life even though it is a secluded life it's my life which I would not change it if I could I write my books which keep me very busy but I like talking either by phone or in person I know one reason I don't have any company is because I smoke cigarettes of course but I don't drink or go to bars since I don't drink or go to bars any more I am more content since I never liked being in a crowd anyway years ago I didn't even go to many if any Family reunions at Christmas or other holidays but I will admit I can feel more at ease in a crowd of people that haven't known me all of my life and dwelling on things that happened 20-30 years ago since the past is just that the past and nobody can change the past for years I knew people that lived in the past and later came back to the present in my almost 51 years I have accomplished many things some of which I am proud of but some which I would like to forget and some of my past I haven't been out of my Apartment much however I could go anywhere I wanted I just feel better here I haven't even gone out to eat since I don't cook I go get me a sandwich and come back here and since I receive my mail here at the Apartment I don't even have to go very far to get my mail which I like plus it actually saves me money where I was spending almost $ 60.00 Sixty Dollars on a Post Office Box for many years I turned the keys into the Post Office and filled out a change of address form plus since I bought some stamps I don't even have to go to the Post Office to mail anything which took a little getting use to since for many years I was use to going to the Post Office getting the mail and mailing whatever too wherever or to whomever it needed to go to plus another thing I love about living here at the Apartment complex is that UPS

United Parcel Service will deliver things to the Office where as when I lived at my Ranch they wouldn't deliver anything to me I had to go to a Store to pick-up the delivery, but living here at the Apartment complex makes it so much easier where as far as my love life I don't have a love life however, but I set here writing my books at my Apartment as I moved into the Apartment complex that Summer the Manager placed some papers in the door to my Apartment one was for getting into the swimming pool area which I didn't even fill out since I can't swim I thought what the fuck would I need to get into the swimming pool area since my passionate writing is my biggest pleasure that and my Cigarettes I must admit that being lonely sucks but since I have spent most of my life alone I prefer living alone to being married since I've been there done that and I'm use to doing things when I get damn good and ready however I would like to meet a Woman to go out with and talk with sometimes but if it happens it does but since I don't go out much I don't look for a Woman too mysteriously appear at my Apartment door I had dreams in the past of traveling some which I could still do if I wanted to but I would never think of traveling now besides I don't know where the fuck would I go anyway I love giving the Woman pleasure anyway possible and I'm not bragging on myself but I know how to please a Woman I know other Men do also but I have a special way of giving a Woman pleasure, my living here at the Apartment complex where I live alone I am not alone plus I feel more secure and more at ease than I ever felt before but I know I will never meet anybody setting here in my Apartment but I live alone by choice and not because I have to before I spend most of my time writing my books since it gives me pleasure plus when I get an idea I put it on my Computer whether it is on a book which I'm writing or another book up to now but since I realized a while back that the person that has always trusted everyone is only asking for pain simply because that most everyone is out for what they can get there are a few people that will help anyone without expecting something in return that is most people I remember one when I lived at my Ranch he would come help me with certain things, but when I was cleaning my barns out and he saw something he could use he would give me not even what something was actually worth of course there was times when I would let him have certain things for helping me but other times I would be needing to make a few extra dollars and got screwed in one way or another but now I never hear from this Man but that all right too but since some good friends helped me move to the City even though since I don't live the most exciting life it's the life I have become use to my setting and writing my books and some people might think my books are explicit I feel that nobody should be ashamed of their sexuality and unless a person is comfortable with their own sexuality a person isn't comfortable just being themselves but the worst thing is acting one way around certain people then another way around other people but I would never do such because not only is it dishonest but it makes the person unable to trust the other person but I am a very private person I don't bother anybody I speak to People but I am not going to pressure anybody to speak I try to speak to everyone when I go out I always think just by saying hello how are you might brighten the persons day or evening since I had a caring and trusting nature about me but now I trust nobody however I do care for some people I care mainly about myself I must say that my life is a happy life however lonely but I enjoy being alone, I have had people tell me to get a life I have always tried pleasing everyone that I came in contact with I have always listened to others say all kinds of things about me or my Family regardless of how pleasant or unpleasant the statement might be but since I have stopped taking shit from people I have to admit I feel pretty damn good I have never gone to visit many people but as I visited a little while I couldn't hardly wait to get back to my Apartment my safe zone as I had a skin cancer on my lip several years ago after I had to have my lip sown back on from a wreck I had where I lost control and hit a tree which threw me from the driver's side to the passenger side after the surgery to remove the cancer after I got me another vehicle I drove down to Beaumont, TX for 6 - 8 weeks if not longer for radiation treatments Monday through Friday after completing all the treatments I went back for check ups when I felt fine but my Parents wanted me to go so I did but after several trips this one Doctor came into the room which I didn't like anyway because every damn time he came in he looked through my shirt pockets and it got to where when I went if he came in I told him I needed to use the Men's room but I left instead since I had already informed the desk of the way he did things but the last time I went the other Doctor wanted me to go into a Hospital which was not going to happen and after a short time I checked with this other Doctor at another clinic he said there was nothing to worry about and that has been years ago and at 50 years old with I have had some good experiences and some not so good because I know everybody has good and bad experiences I will admit that for many years people used me as a doormat in a manner of speaking but not any more my Parents taught me from a very Young age to always be nice to people but not let anyone take advantage of me but I discovered that being nice to some people just opens the door for them to take advantage of that person I have never had the audacity to tell certain people to back off or to get off my back until a while back and I find it tough to say it so I write it in a letter I know that's a kind of chicken shit way out of things but it was easier for me to write a letter than to verbally express myself and I refuse to let people use me as a doormat I for many years wondered how it would feel telling others how I felt about certain things and now I'm able to do just that very thing but living the life of a loner isn't exactly what I wanted of course I didn't imagine that Women would be knocking my door down either since I live in town I go get what I need and come right back here to my Apartment even though I carry my computer with me to where if I have an idea I can enter the idea and then look at it later and if some people talk hell let them talk they probably don't write books' or live life as I do my life is not the most exciting life but it's my life to live. My life is devoted and passionate about my writing my books I know that might sound silly to some but my books are the only thing that I'm passionate about my writing I have always been a passionate person whether it is in a book or in any relationship I put my heart and everything into it I love meeting people and making new friends but it has been my experience that some people are out for what they can get from other people and those that always tried to empress others I will admit several years ago I was one of those people but not any more because I feel if people don't like me for whom I am then fuck them because I am not going to put on an act for anybody and at the same time I am not going to take any shit from anybody either I don't even have a bed in my Apartment since I can't sleep in a bed and haven't been able to for years because of the arthritis in my shoulders plus the fractured vertebra from years ago for years I don't sleep much however when I do wear clean clothes after a hot shower for several years I have felt better sleeping in my clothes I know that might sound silly but that's the way I sleep and either in my recliner or my office chair at my desk where I do my writing on my novels I love my writing even though some people might not but to each their own I am constantly thinking about my next novel setting here smoking another cigarette drinking another cup of coffee or a coke I'm thinking of my next novel I like making a Women feel good about herself and not just through sex but through communicating with her about her needs and listening very closely because in any relationship both the Man and Woman have needs that need to be addressed I don't even drive out by there since it is sold in addition it would bring back painful memories e I lived a loner's life back as I lived at my House in La Porte and when I live at the Ranch also years before I admit that I did go to Night Clubs and get drunk which made things worse even though I knew most everyone there working at the Night Club I got in trouble since I got stopped as I was going home and spent a night in jail and was charged with DWI driving while intoxicated which I will never do again since I love life more since I don't drink any mixed drink or beer even when I'm around People that are drinking and they offer me a beer I say no thank you, if that makes me antisocial then I am antisocial and if they try pushing me then I leave because I don't drink and nobody is going to get me into drinking again I love my life as lonely as it is it is my life and people ask me if I go to shows are something the answer I haven't gone to a show in years one reason is I would have to go alone and I can be alone at my Apartment just as well and I don't do anything Family related since I don't have any Family any more since my Parents died besides both my Sisters have their lives with either their Husbands and kids and grand-kids or kid and grand-kids besides I never went to any Family gathering anyway even when my Dad died I went to the viewing but I couldn't go to the funeral because it would have hurt too much and I remember what my Dad said to me several years if something hurts you too much don't do it of course that was several years before he died but I still remembered that among other things he told me but I just have my life and my books of course I have friends that tell me that I need to get out more which I know but I don't from the fear of either being laughed at or talked about or ridiculed in some way I know that I shouldn't be like that I do go to eat or just drink coffee sometimes just not that much I usually get something to eat and bring it home here to my Apartment to where I can relax and eat in peace some places I have gone to have a screaming kid which I can't take much of that screaming with my writing I am use to talking at places and noise but I do my best writing where it is quite I can write more freely and express myself more openly I use to have a problem expressing myself with others but not any more since it was only hurting myself I am a writer and an author I feel the reason most people treat my like nothing is because I am nothing just a loner that writes books and is a published author many people have said to me that one day I would find true happiness and to me being a loner isn't true happiness but my writing and being a published author does fill some of the void in my life plus the few friends I have to talk too nightly taking a short break from writing then back to my writing on whatever book or books I'm writing at that time ' but now since both Parents are dead I watch after myself now years ago I was falling for every sad story I heard and I would help them out but I soon realized that most of them were laughing their ass off all the way to the bank today I don't help anybody unless I see real need because I can't afford helping that way anyway but I was taught to help people by my Parents but I can't since I live on one check a month and can't work due to my crippled leg of course I still get around and go wherever I want or need to go but I just don't get out much since some not everyone but some people are so cold that you could hang a bag of ice on them and it would never melt that is one reason I am a loner because even though I speak my mind now I could never be as cold or cruel as some people I miss kissing and caressing a Woman's soft skin I know most people would say get married but I've been there done that I admit that I used to set around and cry from being a loner but now I have accepted it as a way of life but I live as a loner and will die a loner but even though it might be a little scary to some people talking about dying but I know that reality plus I am going to make a new will and I even thought about having that put on my head Stone here lays a loner and also in it I feel like putting I want no tears shed at my funeral as I said earlier my life isn't the most exciting life but it's a life which I've live as a loner all of my life fact is I can't remember the time I wasn't a loner even as my Parents were alive of course people seemed to care some but I believe it was just because of my Parents but I am living fine here in my

Apartment although I'm still a loner with a few friends I don't need anybody else in my life and the reason I would ever say such is that I have always been a loner all of my life even though I have set with people and had coffee and talked with them and even had something to eat with them but have never felt comfortable going and visiting anyone at their house I have had people tell me that anytime I wanted to come over was fine but I do have a problem with that because one thing is either I can't smoke around them or they cough outside and say I thought you was going to quit that nasty smoking or by them making a comment about either about my mustache or my hair or something that is really none of their business and my carrying my computers wherever I go for example into a Restaurant or anywhere hell I'm a published Author and not just carrying them for my health and I never know when I might have an idea which I need to put down and the way I feel if they can't understand that it's their problem not mine plus' when I need to either need to put something in a book I'm working on or need to connect to the internet to check something and if others can't understand it then they should keep their mouth shut about it or just not set at the table with me yes I like people but some can be a pain in the ass I have so much on my mind constantly that there has been times when I have gone to a Restaurant to either drink coffee or eat and wanted someone to at least talk to but there have been times when I am writing a new book or putting an idea down when I don't want nobody talking to me and that is one reason I don't go out much but I have written quite a bit in different books as I was setting in a Restaurant and different places and getting new ideas about another book I know some people might find this silly and some might find it strange but even though I am a loner as I am writing a book I don't feel that I am a loner I feel like a very fortunate Man that is able to put things in context making a book out my lonely life but it does piss me off when people push or pressure me to get out more I know that I need to but since I have been hurt so much in the past in one way or another I feel better in my comfort zone here at my Apartment writing my books I know most people can't understand that but I can't help that I am nice to everyone I speak to everyone and if they speak back or not is fine to I am not the Man I used to be one that never expressed himself in the past from fear of hurting someone's feelings but the way I am now I express myself now and if it hurts someone will they will have to get over it or not that is one of the several reasons I don't go out much and continue my writing my books usually I go to Subway and get two party platters to where I will not have to get out much I make sure I have cokes and coffee here or go pick up some mainly to where I can just set and write my books here at my Apartment and I love it today I went to the Office here at the Apartment complex and signed a new Lease because I'm going to live here from now on mainly because I like living here and I know some of the people here and if I moved to a House

I would be not scared but uncomfortable about the neighbors besides I feel at Home here at my Apartment the people that I have met are nice plus I will admit I feel a hell of a lot better and more at ease here than I ever did at my Ranch alone although after my Dad died I felt for some time that I was being watched since I couldn't do anything without someone making some smart ass remarks about my going here or there and finally I after a year or so had to ask the other people that lived there on the Ranch helping my Dad to leave which they did and finally I didn't have like a baby sitter reporting everything to my oldest Sister because every move I made I would get a call asking why I did this or that and fuck I was tired of it besides I was 44 years-old when my Dad died and was grown and everybody needed to get off my ass and stop treating me like a kid besides I had been taught what's right and wrong years ago but I have my life too live as my Sisters have their lives too live and my goal is too live the rest of my life here in peace and quite since I have lived a lone as I've watched and seen others dancing and going on with their lives which I am happy for them but since I live alone I don't want any pity because this is my life and I don't want anybody to come to me saying oh you should do this or that because I've heard all that shit before and a person coming me and trying to make me do something when I don't want too or telling me what I should or shouldn't do or how I should feel a while back I would just put up with it but not any more there has been so many times when I was just setting with someone and they would say some of this shit and it pissed me off and they knew that it pissed me off but I didn't do anything where now if they done that I would give them the finger and say don't take this personally but fuck you I have tried many different things to deal with and overcome my being a loner but with every move I made toward something that I enjoyed it seemed the door was actually closing instead of opening for me at least it always seemed that way to me when some people would say where one door closes another door opens which is true but paths I was on went nowhere or came to a dead end in my pursuit meeting the right Woman there by ending my battle if you want to call it a battle with loneliness which several years ago as I was quite young I had a temper years back as I was coming up which of course I don't now have any temper now since I am a loner plus I have learned to verbalize myself instead of setting there taking another persons insults however there is a couple of people that have insulted me about my carrying my computers in a Restaurant with me and the only reason I haven't already told them off is because the Woman is a close friend of mine but she lives with her ex that has aids I used to go over to his trailer to visit them but I don't any more and I used to meet them at a Restaurant but don't do that anymore either because I have heard them say what are you doing with your computers in here or why don't you leave them in your Jeep and the reason is the batteries would run down in the heat but the main reason I never know when I might have an idea that I need to put down plus I don't know what their problem is besides I am a published author and neither of them have time or what the close friend would like me to write her life's story which is fine but I can't without the proper equipment with me besides this is my life even though it's a life of a loner it's my life but I love meeting people and making new friends but that's as far as it goes because I've been married and never again and I must say that it feels great not having to put up with a bunch of bitching or take me over here or there or do this or do that besides I'm set in my ways of doing things plus neither Woman I was married or lived within the past ever had to work which was my fault because I feared that they would either get hurt or offered a better life to where they didn't have to work since they would be talking with people I believe now that even though people say this and that about my ever being happy I am happy living my life day by day month by month year by year since living the life of a loner is the only type of life I am used too for many years my goal was to make others happy but now since a huge majority of the world doesn't care about anything or anybody it's very hard to be compassionate about others when in return they show none but that is the way the world is but my writing makes my life as content as I ever hope to be since nobody cares, I wish they would stop pretending that they care because there is a name for people like that which is two-faced and I would rather live My life as a loner as I am than to be a friend at their convenience and a nobody when it's not convenient but I never intend to burden anybody the few friends I do have or otherwise I even talk when it's a telemarketer calling me when I use to just hang up I talk to them a few minutes now since at least it is someone to talk with if not but just a few minutes of course unless I'm busy writing, I always trusted people until I realized trusting and believing everything anybody told me was wrong and now today I don't trust anyone since I know that most people not everybody but most will take advantage of people if that person lets them, of course if I see a way I can help a person that actually needs help if I can and only if I can I will help the person as long as it doesn't put me in a bind, but it really hurts when I know that I am being fucked and not even kissed and that is the main reason I don't trust anyone and that is one of my reasons for remaining a loner, of course I still care about certain people but I love life even as a loner since that's the life I have always lived I know some people would say but what about the time your Parents owned the Construction Company well about that when I wasn't out in the shop either working I was in the Office but I knew when people came by the Office it damn sure wasn't there to see me but my Dad or someone else whether it was a sales person or just one of his friends some of which acted like I was in the way where others acted like I didn't exist much less belong there but I will never forget when my Dad needed a file on something the others couldn't find it yet I could go to a file cabinet and get it which I knew pissed others off of course not my Dad he was glad

I knew where to find things plus I know that among other things caused resentment there in the Office, I remember I worked in the shop on big engines even when the other mechanics went home I would go to my House also for a little bit but I went back to finish whatever engine I was working on to where I could do something else the next morning since it never failed that in the morning or at quitting time something else needed some repairs even though I knew some I had watched the other mechanics and was able to do the same plus I asked questions also but this was as I lived in Lomax which is now La Porte before I moved to the Ranch which I inherited but sold due to the incident mentioned earlier, my life has always been a loners life and as I was younger I even cried because I was so lonesome like a record I had on my jukebox I'm so lonesome I could cry of course I had other songs on there also that was as I live in my House in La Porte but now I have accepted it as a way of life, I remember as my Parents were alive people visited them all the time at their house or at the Office but as I moved into the House my Parents had built for me my Parents built one of my Sisters a house across from me which I didn't like since I couldn't move without being asked where I was going are what I was going to do or something either by her or my Parents whom my Sister would call and report my every move too but if I ever questioned anything about her well that was another story all together, between her and the Man with his Family still living at the Ranch after my Dad died I had no privacy at all, my life isn't much of a life but it's my life, I remember the trips my Dad and I took I especially remember one trip as we were going back to the Ranch from a Cattle auction or something he pulled on the shoulder of the highway and told me to get out he said I'm going to whip your ass I set there startled as anyone can imagine as he came to the passenger side of his Truck as he said get over there and drive which I did but it was a shock since he never done anything like that before I miss my Parents my Dad especially because we went many places together I know that is one of the reasons that my Sisters resent me so much but I had a connection with Dad that they didn't plus being the youngest of the Family Dad and I ran our Cattle together which I checked on them to make sure none was having a calf or in the wrong pasture or just to look at them and sometime feed them out of my hand which I really miss that but since I was told that I should sale my Cattle since I owned some personally I sold mine and my Dads Cattle were moved up to another county and sold but the Equipment there at the Ranch which I inherited and was supposed to inherit the Cattle and Equipment also since that was the way my Mother had things in her Will and my Dad stated in his Will that things were to be divided as stated in her Will but it didn't happen that way,

I live a very quite lonely life that most people can't even begin to understand why I live this way but the fact of the matter I have been hurt not so much not physically as much as emotionally and I have always been a very emotional person of course not as much as I once was at one time, I know they say that true happiness comes from within which is very true but different things make different people happy since there is many different types of happiness also there is different types of love and different forms of gratification also, my pleasure was pleasing others in anyway I could but I realized that depending on people only opens a person to be hurt since most people care about their own gratification and fuck everybody else but the type of Man that I am unless I can give a Woman some gratification at least in someway of course after she and I had known each other a while, I knew this one Woman a while as I lived on my Ranch she came down to visit a few times she even cleaned my House but this one day she came down and she really didn't feel like working since she had been up all night she lived with her ex but he didn't care for her anymore or that is what I was told, I was introduced to her by this Man that cut some tree after a bad storm had uprooted some and had taken many others down also but on the day she wasn't feeling good I had her lay down on my sofa I could tell she was very tensed from being up all night I gave her a massage and as I was massaging her clothes kept getting in the way of my giving her a good relaxing massage so I said to her those clothes keep you from relaxing why not take them off she was shocked for a few minutes and I said you do not have to worry I'm not going to do anything so she undressed as she got down to her panties I said hey take them off to where you can completely relax which she did as she laid down I massaged her from head to toe then had her roll over as I massaged her back as I talked very softly to her letting her know that I nor anybody was going to hurt her of course it was just me and her there and I moved down her back to the cheeks of her ass massaging the cheeks of her ass down her thighs both inner and outer thighs massaging her legs feet and toes talking very softly and before I even finished she was sound asleep I went to get a blanket to cover her up with as I covered her body she curled up like a baby with her favorite blanket she slept for several hours she had told me before that she needed to be at home by four because her Daughter got home at four I went and woke her up a little before four o'clock as she was stretching from her sleep I said her I want to give you something as I inserted some fingers inside her pussy as she said I need to get home then she relaxed again as I moved my fingers in and out up and down inside her juicy pussy and I gave her not one not two but three orgasms just with working my fingers inside her as I removed my fingers I went to wash my hands as she followed to clean herself as she got dressed and I took her back home I said hey I know I'm just a dirty old Man and she shocked me as she said a very special dirty old -Man I seen her a few times after that then I never seen her again of course that one time was the only time I pleased her,

T hen one night as I was online I met another Woman we communicated through chatting online then by phone then as we met and hugged and kissed I almost felt like going back home then but I thought I would see what happened and if she warmed up at least a little as we went to eat we talked some about her dead husband then the weather got bad as we went back to her House where she changed back into her shorts that she was wearing as we met which I saw nothing wrong with that, I liked her and I thought she liked me but as we decided to stay there and watch a movie since she had several movies but as we began watching the movie since I hadn't been out in years I asked if I could kiss her as I did I could tell that she really wasn't that excited about my being there plus the way she went outside to smoke quite a bit as I went out to smoke with her I asked her if there was anything wrong and she said nothing of course as I went out to be with her she went to turn the movie off after the movie we walked outside were we hugged and kissed and I left as I got home I looked online were I noticed an email from her I think it was that night or the next day I received the email that told me that I reminded her of her dead husband which was a slap in the face to me and then she said that she enjoyed my company since she told me earlier that nobody came to visit her either but I stayed in contact with her and one time when I called she had company which I told her that I understood after some time had passed I called again but this time there was no dogs barking in the back-round the evening I was there she had her dogs all 8-9 of them in the House which I understood to a certain extent for protection but I never expected to spend more time petting her dogs since I went to be with her, but that was the last time I talked with her, my live as a loner has had more ups and downs than a yo-yo and more downs than ups and since I have always live a life of a loner I like meeting people and making new friends but most people don't have time or say that for an excuse but most people not all but most just don't care about anything or anyone but themselves and even though I might not be the only lonely person in the world it sure as hell feels like it again I use to always please others at my expense with no more of that shit either, I feel that a friend should be a friend and not just a friend when they need something plus a friend is someone you can trust and I don't know of many people that I actually trust, it's pretty hard trusting many people when you have been shit on by many people in the past which is why I stay at my Apartment at least most of the time to think and meditate on what my next subject will be to write about whether it is fiction or non- fiction it gives me pleasure to write, plus writing relaxes me, I am sure that writing might not sound peaceful to some people but to me it is quite peaceful, another thing that burnt my ass is years ago as I was I my 40's as I either went somewhere with someone or they went with me especially one person wanted me to set by him and never move which wasn't going to happen we were at a casino we both played the slots but when one didn't pay anything after putting some money in it I moved around because I wasn't going to continue putting my money in if I didn't get some back, what irritated me is that even though I lost the first six years of my life it was no excuse for the friends or so I thought were my friends to treat me with no respect plus treating me like a kid always smothering me when I felt like telling them to fuck off though I didn't though I didn't since I'm quite sure my Parents had something to do with it also, but now since my Parents died and at one time I had to tell off my oldest Sister and Brother- in-law letting them know I don't need another Mother and Dad since I was feeling smothered again and not in so many words I was telling them to leave me the fuck alone, living alone is the only life I've ever known which really sucks but that's the way it is plus I don't really know any other way to live since this is what I have been accustomed too, I am the type of Man that if I had not just a friend but a real friend a friend that would be a friend no matter what, a friend to turn to day or night and you could call on those nights when you couldn't sleep a friend you could trust, one that would understand the pain or suffering caused by others, believe me I know how much heartache pain and suffering others so called friends can cause I been there, a true friend is a friend through good times and bad and don't lie that is one of the things that really burns my ass is when anyone especially a Woman lies to me and with no cause or explanation why, I would rather her slap me or just tell me to fuck off or something just don't lie to me be honest and open that's all I ask of anyone, I guess I care to much for people but I am not like most people I care about people but I don't expect every Woman I care about to just jump in bed and say here I am do with me what you will, however loving someone is a totally different thing, now the only person I love is myself since other people have continued playing their games say I love you too and all the time know that they didn't mean a word of it or telling a person that you will be somewhere and never showing up or calling this is one of the reasons I don't trust anyone because other people let me down so much I believe someone is going to meet me when I see the whites of their eyes I know people that say that I shouldn't be like that but when I can't trust people to do what they say I mean hell what else am I supposed to do, most young people get marry not for love but most of them marry from being in heat of course the same happens with older people also but just not as often as with young people then everybody might wonder why the divorce rate is so high in America but the main reason older people get married is out of loneliness but at 50 years old I am so used to being alone plus set in my ways of doing things I don't know whether anyone could stand being married to me since I can't work due to my crippled leg and if she worked I would constantly fear her finding someone that could offer more than I can but since none of my ex-wives worked of course I was making a weekly salary back as my Parents were alive also but now it's once a month from a trust-fund my Dad set-up before he died, now on pleasing a Woman I would say that at least 50 % maybe higher or lower of Men don't know how to please a Woman the way to please a Woman is to actually spend time with her and for the Woman's sake forget about thinking that just because you the Man got your rocks off don't mean she is satisfied by a long shot, spend time touching & caressing and kissing her soft skin and getting her wet not just a little bit the wetter you get them the more they will like making love this is why most Woman leave home and their Husbands among other reasons I'm sure but if they don't get the love and attention instead just quicky every once in a while she is going to leave Men just think about it like this if a Woman got you to a certain point where you were about to get your rock off and just before she went to the restroom think how you Men would feel I'm sure you would be mad just think about how she feels when she don't experience an orgasm she feels used like just another piece of ass, if you Men really love her then show your love forget the flowers or roses for now the pleasure she wants is her Man to respect her as she respects your requests when most Men want a Woman to go down on them the Woman does it without hesitation but the Man going down on her the Man would say oh that is nasty but think your Woman just let you get your rock off in her mouth and in fairness she deserves the same pleasure where most Men say well I just can't do that then why do you think she enjoys going down on you most Men would say she does that because she loves me, the Woman does whatever she can do to please her Husband and some Women endure pain without saying anything to their Husbands and most Men don't know the pain they inflicted on the Woman because of silence fearing that if she divorces the Husband that inflicts pain on her she fears that no other Man will want her but if she stays with him or goes back to him she does not respect herself nor does she respect those that love her it's like it takes a bigger Man to walk away from a fight than to stand there and fight turn it around and a Woman shows more respect for herself and others if she says I'm not taking anymore shit, remember it's better to be alone than to be abused or the Woman standing there taking it and ending up in the Hospital or worse dead every Woman deserves to be treated with respect and like a Woman and not just as a sex object, most Men expect a Woman to take care of the kids if they have kids plus cook, clean and to have sex whenever the Man or her Husband gets ready which is nothing but using her as a slave and a whore or sex slave which is so wrong what if the rolls were reversed how would you

Men feel what the hell is the difference most Men would say but I work all day or whatever which is no excuse for not showing her more attention and by attention I don't mean hitting or slapping her I mean showing her that you truly love her and if by kissing, caressing her soft skin and giving her multiple orgasms getting her extremely wet how you Men might ask gently inserting your fingers inside her vagina (pussy) moving them in and out very slowly getting her not only wet but drenched will show her that you care if you really do care for her and don't tease her with doing this once and never doing it again of course there are several ways to get her wet but just don't tease her besides you the Men wouldn't like it if a Woman was teasing you, if you the Men don't care about her don't be mean and cruel to her because you wouldn't like it if they were mean and cruel too you physically or sexually and if she wants to leave Men don't fight it because it's better to be alone than to be with someone that doesn't love you I know that things end badly are else they wouldn't end but when and if you see each other again at a Store or anywhere you don't have to carry on a conversation but just to say hello and how are you doesn't mean that you want to have an affair with her again it is just showing that there are no hard feelings and even if it were so except and move on with life but at least you can speak to each other, I must say this will not only make you the Men feel better but the Woman as well especially if there are kids involved, most Women would never admit the level of attention that they need that shows a

Woman that you care and if they can't get it one way they will try another way almost to the point of seduction but of course when a Woman has been married to a Man for any length of time and he doesn't pay any attention to her except in bed she is going to try to get his attention one way or another but if he shows no interest she has every right to leave him in pursuit of someone that will give her the attention she needs both in and out of bed, Women require more attention than Men of course not twenty-four seven but more than just the time in bed where after making love the Man rolls over and goes to sleep which is wrong because if every time the two of you meaning the Man and Woman are in bed that is all no talking at all about anything the Woman will feel like a whore maybe just the Husbands whore but still a whore just the same, if you love her and care about her as a Husband is supposed to love his Wife there is no excuse for ever treating her like a whore, so a word of advice to you Men that are married talk to your Wife about things that interest her and not just about sexual things I'm sure you could find out more about her if you just listen to her and to the Man thinking about getting married marriage to a two way commitment if you can't communicate with her instead of going out every night with the other guys either to play games or to drink or whatever then afterwards going home and expecting your Wife to meet your every desire or to meet him at the door or in the bedroom knowing she is going to either have to fuck and act like she enjoys it or get abused or maybe both and the sad part is that the Woman never reports this some say it's out of fear or say it's out of love that's not love letting your Husband beat you till your bruised all over or worse sexually abusing you, the Wife who does everything she can to please him with no complaints whatsoever and afterwards he says go get me a beer and shut your crying up unless you want some more and the Wife goes and gets him the beer he asked for or cook him something to eat even though you the Wife don't feel like it you do it out of fear he might hurt you worse than he already has and if as the Husband comes home as the Wife is just asking where he has been he might say it's none of your fucking business or beating her just for asking after most Husbands sober- up most not all Husbands say how sorry they are as they caress the bruises they done to their Wife the night before in a drunken rage of course there are Men that might not even drink that beat their Wives, many Husbands think that just because they are mad about whatever something that happened at work or just anything instead of going for a ride and cooling off they take it out on the closest person to them which is their Wife who is supposed to be a life long partnership commitment between the Man and Woman but however it doesn't always work out that way some Men think that just because they are married to a Woman it gives them control over them right but they are wrong because a marriage certificate does not give the Man control of the marriage or the Woman, in a marriage a Man and Woman share responsibilities but the main responsibility for the Woman is herself there are Women that think that their main responsibility is to keep their Man happy wrong if the Woman can't be happy in the relationship she needs to get out of it of course there will be good and bad times but that just life but there is no reason living a life full of fear never knowing when he might hurt you externally or internally and life is to be enjoyed not to be abused nothing gives the Man the right to abuse the Woman and yes I know that Men would say but we have the right WRONG nobody in this world has the right to abuse another person besides that isn't love that's trying to control and marriage does not give any Man control over a Woman, the Men need to realize this before getting married unless the Man can promise to love and protect the Woman of their dreams and companion of their lives but of course the Man is giving 100% it's over before it really begins the reason I say the Man giving his 100% is because the Woman give their 100% by keeping things in order around the House keeping it clean making sure you have clean clothes to wear & cooking the meals plus going down on you whenever you want her too and to tink that there are Men that still never think about all the things she does for you as your either at work or off with the guys where it is actually work and the Woman never complains and sometimes she feels like leaving because she does not get the appreciation for all that she does but she doesn't say anything she just tries to please her Man but a question is when was the last time you the Man really pleased her no not by fucking her but truly pleased her by either going down on her or kissing, licking and sucking her complete body front and back and when was the last time she experience a orgasm most Men don't even know when the last time their Woman or Wife had an orgasm most would say well I think it was a week ago but Men think about it you if you care about the relationship at all you should meet her needs also since both you and her are married or thinking about getting married remember a Woman has sexual needs also where most Men think of just their own gratification but again some Men seem like they don't care which is wrong and the Women deserve better and I tell you Men what's pitiful is when the Woman has to turn to another means to satisfy herself which is BOB her battery operated buddy her vibrator for pleasure since some Men think that the Women is either living with you or married to you just to give you pleasure wrong again and Men when was the last time you made the Woman in your life feel special? I know most of you would say I buy her things but that's not enough one way to make your Woman feel special is to either take a shower with her without expecting her to put out or to give you a blow job there in the shower or another way is as she is drawing bath water go and help her into the bathtub and with a wash cloth gently soap her body then rinse her off and help her out of the bathtub and gently dry her body from her head to her toes kissing each part of her body as you gently wipe it dry with a bath towel it will show her that you care about her and not only about getting you having her give you a blow job every time you do something for her, this will show her that you care if you do care about her, then kissing and caressing her soft skin as both of you either lay on the bed or after she puts on some panties and a night gown going to set in a chair or on the sofa then surprising her by gently massaging her entire body from head to toe kissing her entire body as you massage her talking to her in a very soft seductive voice letting her know that your not going to hurt her nor will you let anyone else hurt her showing her the pleasure of true love and passion as she awakes telling her that you love her if in fact you do then show her by gently moving one side of her panties to other side and gently insert your fingers in her vagina moving your fingers all around inside her nice wet vagina making her wetter and wetter by doing so you will be showing her that you care about her being happy also she will probably say oh my god as she is experiencing orgasm, but don't stop there by leaving your soaked fingers with her cum inside her moving your fingers around and around inside her wet vagina with her experiencing multiple orgasms without her having to please the Man at the same time even though it might shock her at the same time she will be pleasantly surprised by your actions besides Men there is a lot of difference in sex with a Woman and making love to a Woman, the difference having sex with a Woman is just that sex and shows no respect to the Woman whatsoever and Men if you have no more respect for your Woman or Wife then you don't need to be married however if the Man really love and cares about his Woman he will take his time and make love but before always remember that foreplay is one of the most important parts of making love and if you really love and care for her you will take time or make time to get her wet and the wetter you get her vagina before making love the better, so just remember the wetter the better plus the Woman will never forget it either, most Men would say well I can't do that and I would say why the hell not the Woman does things that she would rather not do to please the Man for example as the Woman is sucking the Mans cock if the Man asks her to insert a finger up his ass the Woman does it to please the Man without any hesitation, the Man should be just as receptive to her needs as she was to his needs instead of his thinking that she is there just to please him any relationship between a Man and a Woman has to be a two way street and can't be self-centered because if it is the Woman will think hey I could have done this with BOB her battery operated buddy, I don't mean to brag but each time I am with a Woman and make love I don't think of my pleasure as much as I think of ways to give her pleasure and by giving her pleasure I receive pleasure from giving her pleasure and whether we make love or not I give her multiple orgasms I feel that if asked in a private survey how many Woman experienced a true orgasm with someone else in the room such as their Husband I feel not many if any Women would be able to put that they had experienced true orgasm each time with their Husbands where some Men don't care or don't seem to care, by caring I am saying being as gentle as possible with her when she needs your attention don't just blow her off because that is showing her that you don't respect her and without respect you the Husband have no compassion or love for her whatsoever which is a good sign that you and her should divorce before it turns into the abuse cycle because no Husband has the right to abuse the Woman, they married for better or worse and I know that in any relation there will be good and bad times since I've been there done that but I never abused any Women that I was married or lived with I got in my vehicle and left to cool off where sometimes I would realize that it really wasn't a big fucking deal to begin with, but there were times when I had to get them out of my life since they tried to run my life also when they couldn't even run there own or so it seemed they either had their Parents or their so called friends telling them what to do about anything and I wasn't going to put up with that shit at all because I was married to the Woman not her Family or friends however if either her Family or friends wanted to suggest something I would listen but it was up to me whether I want to take the advice or not besides opinions are like ass holes everybody has one, my life even as empty and lonely as it is it's my life to live here at my Apartment living the life of a loner, another thing is when others have said that they know what I've been going through is a line of shit because unless a person has been lonely as long as I have there is no fucking way they can say that they know or understand what I'm going through my life isn't much but it's my life, my life even several years ago back when I lived in La Porte and moved to the Ranch where I live until the House that I lived in where I was assaulted was a lonely life and many people even today can't understand how I can stand living alone but I will say this since I've spent most of most of my life alone even when some pretended like they cared I could tell that deep down inside the only person they cared about was themselves which is fine because some of the people I've been close to have caused me so much pain that I stay in my Apartment most of the time where I don't have to deal with the lyes and deception of other people but after being deceived by hell just yesterday a Man said he was going to deliver a item which I had purchased from a store but I waited and waited and I done something I never done before I called and told them that I had changed my mind and decided not to get the item as I went to the store where I met the manager of the store where I told him that I was there to get my money back from the item I had purchased a few days ago as I explained my displeasure since I still had not received the item he said that this other Man could deliver it which was fine but I explained to him and the other Man the dishonored promise that the Man would deliver it that day but as I was talking the Man that was supposed to deliver the item walked in and was saying things about his Truck which I already heard about when I called the store that he was having problems with it but damn it was Friday and if I didn't get the item delivered then I was sure I would have had to wait until Monday which wasn't going to happen even there in the store he apologized which I ignored but as he delivered the item he still apologized which I excepted and said that I understood but at the store talking to the manager I told him and the other Man that he should at least called me which they agreed with, several years ago I would have never called asking for my money back and going to the store raising hell but now I changed in the way I do things most people think that they can continuously put me off think that I will never say or do anything like my Dad would always let people get by with that shit but not me this is why I don't trust many if any people since some people not all but some will be verbally stab a person in the back and/or cut you down which I have put up with my entire life I remember one time as my Parents owned the Construction Company a sales person came to the Office one day to talk with my Dad and I was setting in the Office at the time the sales person from a Company gave me a cap that said the Company name which he worked for VIP which I appreciated my Dad had bought quite a bit of Equipment from the Company this sales Man worked for but later that day I was wearing the cap in the Office and I was degraded by a person there in the Office I know he was trying to be something as he saw the cap he said so VIP huh very important pussy which was very degrading to say but I didn't say anything I just went on back to mine and my Dads Office but I knew the reason was because me and my Dad were close as each Family has young people that are closer to one parent than the other of course loving both Parents but just feeling closer to either Mom or Dad I remember all the trips me and my Dad went on whether it was going deer hunting or to visit relatives out of town or going to Cattle auctions where I met quite a few people where I met people such as Nolan Ryan and Leroy Jordan and others as I was in the Beefmaster Breeders Universal and the Beefmaster is a cross between the Shorthorn and Hereford type Cattle, which I am no longer in since I was forced to sell my Cattle and Bulls years ago and my Dad's Cattle and Bulls also although my Dad's which I was to inherit were taken to another County and sold the Cattle and since my Dad had everything paid for meaning the Ranch and the Cattle and the Equipment things that I was supposed to inherit with the Ranch but the Bank over the Trust at that time didn't see thing's like that but what really hurt was when the auctioneer came to my Ranch and went into the barns with his Men and said this goes and that goes and they took the items over on the other side of my property there at my Ranch and auctioned the items and Equipment off, but now my Trust fund is with another Bank which I'm so glad of, I have always dreamed of sharing my life with a beautiful Woman but some years ago I realized that my hopes and dreams were just that hopes and dreams that could never happen since I had so much ripped from my life and I began thinking what the hell if I met the Woman of my dream would I have to offer her besides myself and my love and affection and I know that a relationship requires more but that is all I have to offer a Woman of course with incredible nights, but I know that is not enough plus I am to set in my ways for a Woman to really become interested or involved with me anyway I feel my chances of that happening are very unlikely, this is my main reason for remaining a loner I know most people would say but you have a few friends I would say yes but one of the hardest things is when I'm talking to a friend on the phone is saying bye since not knowing if I will hear from that person tomorrow or next week or next month or ever, but of course I know that they have jobs and other things to do or just to busy or just don't care which is the category that most people fall under the categories to busy or don't care and since I'm not letting people walk all over me I might not have many if any friends but friends don't walk all over friends, life is a lonely life with everyone being so busy that they can't take a minute to call and say hello or just not caring about anything or anybody because they are wrapped up in their own world but if they ever experience the lonely world a loner lives in both day and night most people would wonder what the fuck is this if everybody lost interest in what you were doing at work and instead of bringing you projects they gave them to others knowing it would take twice if not three times as long for them to complete the project, where if they gave you the project it would be done within half the time you would feel rejected and if you tried calling someone you had known for years yet they constantly said that they didn't have time to talk at that time but said they would call you back and you waited and waited for a call back but the phone never rang which happens quite often with me but that's ok too or setting and waiting for someone to come visit and after waiting and waiting the person never shows and you think what the fuck is this shit then you get to thinking is it me because I am nice to everybody or is it because I smoke or that my Apartment smells like smoke where some people go outside to smoke with my crippled leg I can't go outside and stand around just to smoke my cigarettes besides it is getting to where that is about the only place you can smoke at a persons Home or Apartment, as I lived at my Ranch I stayed in the House after my Dad died and wrote my books and smoked my cigarettes and if somebody came that didn't like smoke or my smoking I felt like telling them to get the fuck out of course I didn't especially if they were there to help me with some project or something as I mentioned before like this one Man he would always cough just around me and say I though you were going to quit that nasty smoking of course when someone would come over to help me with a Computer I didn't smoke out of respect for them and here at my Apartment if a person doesn't smoke like the Insurance agent that came over I didn't smoke until she left I try to be considerate of other people but there is times I know the more considerate a person is the more they expect also, where I was a while back always giving trying to make others happy no more of that shit either when the fuck is my turn to receive besides constantly giving to others with might or might not appreciate the help anyway, it seems that most people act especially the Women that I personally am like he other Men out there but I am not of course I have needs just like any other Man but I don't push or pressure her in anyway shape or form because unless the Man and Woman can enjoy just being together without any sexual contact then no relationship will last even when a Man is going out or dating a Woman no Woman is just jump at meeting a Man's every need without her needs being met also, I must admit I have had my share of I didn't want to say it but my share of prick teasers also but a Man has to restrain his sexual urges or just saying anything to a Woman because they could call that sexual harassment where if the Man tells a Woman how beautiful she is they take that as a complement but if the Man that just comes out and tells a Woman that she looks good enough to eat the Man has no scruples about himself, I know one Man that asked a Woman what makes a Man's dick get hard and right in a Restaurant I felt like leaning over and slapping him but didn't, the Woman answered him since she knew this Man and which I used to drink Coffee with him everyday but don't anymore he was a Womanizer or that is what he wanted everybody to think anyhow, as I mentioned earlier that I like meeting people and making new friends which I don't pursue that very often since most people just don't care about anything or anybody but themselves anymore and don't seem to have time to get to know one another and the way I feel now if a person is embarrassed to be seen with me or embarrassed by the way I am dressed at least I'm clean, I always look at things if a person don't want to get to know me then it her loss, I received a call one evening from a Woman which I didn't even answer because as we met I felt like she wanted to be somewhere else hell she even told me that I was keeping her from her nap which I apologized for which I didn't have to but I did anyway she was a beautiful Woman which I was honored to meet her and I care about her however when she made that statement about my cheating her out of her nap I wasn't sure but it was a joke, I stayed there talking with her for about four hours where we enjoyed the meeting each other I enjoyed meeting her as we first met she kissed me before we went into the establishment and before she left I kissed her, I enjoy talking with her every night but it is at the point where we run out of things to say to each other, but with her strong Family ties which I respect that, but I feel unless we can spend more time together not intimately or by phone actually together the most it could ever be is a friendship which is fine, I know she is trying to move into a Apartment to where she can claim her independence again which I understand, this is the story of my life as a loner which is no life at all and people ask why not get out more take chances like everybody else since I've always been a loner my Apartment is my safe zone I feel better in my safety zone and writing my books plus because I feel even though I am more verbal about things that bother me as people say and do things and if they get mad they either have to live with it or get over it, I live a quite lonely life some might call it a boring life but writing my books makes my life more content since this is the way I have always lived my life as a loner I don't know any other lifestyle that I would even consider, my childhood was everything but normal since I had already been through so damn much and even in School where I was in the regular classes I never had any friends and even at recess I was off by myself since everyone else was either talking about going over to somebody's house after School and spending the night or something I guess the thing about School was that I was used to being around adults even though I had two Sisters that were in School although different grades they were always telling me what to do I guess that's why I didn't stay married to neither one of my Wife's very long at all or live with a live-in either because it seemed to me that they pulled the pants off of me and put them on themselves like they were running the show and that dog wasn't going to hunt at least with me I was working and coming home sometimes to a empty House and other times to just a bunch of bitching take a shower to where we can eat go help my Dad work on his Truck where I spent my money for whatever parts were needed to get the Truck running again the Truck was a Freightliner which I didn't mind but damn I was working for my Dad's Construction Company during the day and working on her Dad's haul

Truck at night at a Truck yard in another City, as I divorced her I had been going to a one of the Restaurant's in La Porte where I met this Woman that I liked after a little we got married which didn't last long either but the problem was once a month she would say that she needed to sleep in another bedroom which I fell for that line of shit but not for long since she was talking to someone one the phone late at night and then took one of her trips out of town she said to see her Parents but then she said it was to see her Sister but I knew what she was doing but I was waiting for her to tell me which never happened but the shocked look that was on her face one evening as I got Home after she had returned from one of her trips as I walked in I said I want a divorce she said what you don't love me anymore and I said no I don't she said well it's going to take me a few days to find some place to live which I fell for and I lived out at the Office when I could have gone to my Parents or got a Motel room but I didn't since I thought she would be gone in a few days but I was wrong she stayed there I forget how long but my Dad went over and told her to get out which she did after I divorced her after a months I forget how long out of loneliness I went back to the one that expected me to keep her Dad's haul Truck going but after just a very short time within months I divorced her again which showed me that I was supposed to be alone and always being alone still sucks I have excepted it as a way of life, I searched and searched for that one thing to fill the void in my life when in 2002 I thought about writing to fill some of the void in my life however there is still some void in my life which I imagine will be buried with me when I die, I like writing not only because it gives my something to do but I like writing, when I'm with a Woman I like making her feel good I like massaging her entire body if she wants me to with no expectations of her sexually or otherwise however I love making love with a Woman but I would never say that she owed me after I made her feel good I am not that type of Man that requires pay back, I like making a Woman feel good through orgasm also with no sex involved to is my way that shows the Woman that she does not have to worry about anything because I would never force a Woman into anything which she wasn't comfortable with, yesterday I was with a beautiful Woman we sat and watched a movie we both liked then we frenched kissed a little while we were watching the movie as we finished watching as she said she was hungry and she said she really didn't want to go out I had already picked up some sandwiches from a local sandwich shop the other day and had picked up her favorite drink or so I thought but before I went to lead her over here to my Apartment I went and picked up her favorite drink and brought them here placed them in the refrigerator to where they would be nice and cold when she wanted one, even though I gave her directions on how to get to my Apartment I thought hey instead of her getting lost and irritated plus it would have cut the time we could spend together in half that's the reason I went and showed her the way over here to my Apartment, as the movie ended we talked a little about things but never about anything sexual which might have or might not have either surprised or shocked her but the truth of the matter is I haven't been intimate with a Woman in 6 -7 years, I pleased a Woman not so long ago but not by making love or having sex with her but through giving her multiple orgasms which gave both me and her pleasure which I talked about earlier, yesterday as I had the Woman at my Apartment even though I felt like I could done almost anything but didn't try anything out of respect for her plus I would rather cut myself with a knife rather than hurt her in anyway shape or form and chance losing what we have between us, we had a good discussion about things between us one night over the phone where I asked her about her past relationships and she told me about one wanting to dominate her every move one which was an alcoholic one was addicted to online pornography sites and chats then one was caught cheating with another Woman which she was engaged to at the time then she met me a Man like she never dreamed possible who could sense when she was nervous and tensed about anything the evening at my Apartment as we watched a movie I placed my hand on her leg but when I sensed her getting nervous I moved my hand I am sensitive to a Woman's being nervous and/or tensed around me but with what she had been through in the past I completely understand her reluctance of trusting any Man after she explained her past relationships I understood her resistance from any involvement with any Man since she has been hurt so many times before, I've always believed if you love someone let them go by not suffocating them if they come back their yours forever but if not it was never yours to begin with, to me that would be dominating her every move, where one was an alcoholic which like some alcoholics abuse their Wife and one that cared more about satisfying his own needs online instead of pleasing his Wife, then the one that was cheating with another Woman and was engaged at the same time, which shows me that none of the Men loved her or respected her a person of course time changes things but no Man has the right to just say or do as they damn well please and if the Wife want to go out like with her Sister or the other Women from work there would be hell to pay, which isn't right because being married to a Man or Woman doesn't give him or her the right to control your every move, some Men think they or superior to Women and vise versa, another reason I am the way I am is because my Parents hardly ever visited anybody of course they visited their Brothers and Sisters or would have them come over to my Parents most of the time except on Christmas then a Family reunion for years at someone's house which I went to a few but not many because I didn't like being in crowds and my Parents and Sisters never understood that but I just didn't like being around a crowd and especially on Christmas morning as everyone opened their presents so I would go and get mine and open mine the night before and nobody understood why but that was the reason why I did it like that it wasn't that I couldn't wait it's that I just had a hard time with everybody saying isn't that cute or making some remark and then everyone would go and might not see each other till next Christmas or else I would go to School as my Sisters would also of course different grades in School as my Mother would stay at Home and my Dad would run his Construction Company which I worked at as I got on the O. J. T. Program out of High School since I had some fights in High School which I liked working for my Dad then after a while I started doing mechanic work for him and I done a little on the side also I remember one evening setting at my House in La Porte a Man called me needing some work done on his trailer which I went to where it the Tractor Trailer was at since it was 8:00 in the evening I couldn't get any parts for it but I thought he had the parts or that's what I understood him to say anyway but he didn't have anything he got a ride to go get the parts needed but instead of that he went somewhere I guess to sleep and I couldn't have left if I wanted to because the Police came and told me to stay there with the rig which I did all night long then the owner of the Tractor Trailer rig showed up with some others to get it fixed as the Trailer was jacked up as I and others was working on it one of my jacks slipped and part of the Trailer almost fell right on me a Police Man knew I had been there since last night but as it fell he told me to get out from underneath that which I did, but as it was fixed I forget how much I charged the owner hell since I couldn't leave since the Police told me to stay there I stayed, but that was several years ago it has been several years I haven't done any mechanic work but due to my crippled leg and age I can't get in the positions I use to as I worked on heavy Equipment, I know which everybody that worked for my Dad thought was a joke but for years that's what I done but then there were times I would go to the Office at night and instead of doing any mechanic work I familiarized myself where everything was meaning the files on the jobs and Equipment everything although my Parents couldn't understand why I was out there at nights since the Secretary or Secretaries done all the book work but since I knew where thing were at sometimes my Dad needed a file on something out of a cabinet and the Secretary couldn't find it yet I could go to the filing cabinets and got exactly what my Dad wanted even though I knew it pissed them off in the front Offices since I didn't have a personal life and they did I knew where things were at as everybody was at home doing god only knows what I was at the Office and even though I was the Office joke I could find things where other's couldn't, of course I had a temper back then also which I wasn't using to get attention but nobody ever around the Office treated me with any respect and I was the bosses son, as I use to say the sob (son of the boss) I went after parts for the Equipment and things which made me the gopher go for this go for that for years once I went from La Porte to Houston three times in one day after parts and got the wrong part each time not because I didn't know what I was going for but they just gave me the wrong part which they finally corrected their mistake, for years I done this to save money and I met a lot of people also but at the end of the day I went to eat then went Home to an empty House where I cleaned up and watched television and slept and then went back to the same thing even though everybody at the Office treated my like I didn't matter of course my Parents didn't but other's treated me like shit even though I helped them anyway possible I was a nothing then and still nothing today and people say get a life I have a life lonely life and not much of a life but it's a life just the same of course back then I was always trying to help people and didn't want to hurt anybody's feelings or anything but now I changed because people don't care about my feelings anymore than they would care about a stray dog or cat the only one they care about is themselves and I remember a time when people cared about each other and at least tried to show some feelings for other people but not anymore, everyone rushes through life trying to do this and that then they notice hey I rushed myself for years and never really took time to enjoy myself in life and then they think oh but I want to get ahead of things but they never think that a person never gets ahead of things if a person thinks so they are only fooling themselves, rushing their lives away, but living one day at a time and changing the things you can and the things you can't just let it happen because life goes on through good time and bad, but through my life I have experienced that depending on others to make me happy is asking for the impossible, so I don't depend on anybody just myself since I'm not going to let myself down but others will and people can and will cause others pain and anguish sometime they act like that don't know when in fact they do it's just they don't care, it burns my ass when people that I've known for years act's like a friend for a while and then when you need help they don't have time or they are to tired which shows that I have no friends which is a painful reality which sucks but I'll live, I have few acquaintances and a few friends yet I live the life of a loner which is the only type of life I've ever really known and my love life I have no love life nor do I have a life in most peoples eyes, I feel better when I'm alone as stated earlier when I do go out either to eat or just drink coffee since due to what was said in the past I don't even go out to much because I would have to tell certain people to mind their own fucking business people I have known for years, that know I'm a author yet they always say something about my taking my computers where ever I go but I do because if I have an idea I'm able to put it down where if I have to go get my computers out of my Jeep of wait till I get back here I usually forget the idea that I wanted to put on paper, for years I never had anyone saying anything I don't know but the people that say things might be wanting me to say something to them but I just haven't because they have a bigger problem I don't,

I like helping Women feel good anyway possible even though the last Woman I had living with me was the last intimate experience which was 6-7 years ago which I knew she enjoyed since I gave her multiple orgasms not only as we made love but the foreplay before actually making love was my way of showing her that I loved her and cared about her plus I remember as we were at the Ranch and was getting out the Truck I remember before I was inside the House she had my shirt unsnapped and my jeans almost to my knees when I said my god can't you wait till we get inside she said well I want you now, I remember we making love in a pasture of course we were inside my Truck but as mentioned before she and I were only together a few months, I have been in pain since that assault in March and I have read up on the pain that I'm going through which I can't understand since I was setting in my Office chair sleeping as the assault took place their at my Ranch which I sold and I haven't even been down in that area again since I moved into my Apartment where I live the same type of life I was living at my Ranch but without the headaches of having to have someone come out and mow the front 40 acres well it was almost 40 acres since the Equipment was auctioned off as well as the Cattle leaving me not even a Tractor to mow the front and pond pasture with and when I asked the Bank that was over my Trust at that time about mowing they said that I would have to rent a Tractor to mow which was bullshit in my opinion but I don't have to worry about that anymore thank god, I am writing again which I have always loved writing which is my one true passion since most people either turn their backs as I'm talking to them or they began talking with someone else as I try telling them something it shows they have no respect whatsoever for me or for what I have to say then when I get their attention again when they ask now what was it that you were trying to say I tell them oh nothing don't worry about it, this is my reason for saying what I said before the reason people treat me like I'm nothing is because I'm nothing, I love my life even though I live the life of a loner which as previously mentioned is the only type of life I known, but the attitude I have know is different than what it used to be since most people don't care about hurting my feelings then it's nonsense my almost walking on egg shells around them trying not to hurt their feelings besides talk is just words although sometimes they hurt people they get over words but physically assaulting someone is jail offense, so the next time someone says or does something to hurt my feelings instead of letting it build up I'm going to speak up besides not speaking up is only hurting me, opinions are like ass holes everybody's got one, it really gets me the way some Men can go and tell in very intimate details what they done with their Wife because it shows no respect for his Wife or Woman, the way some Men can go off where ever they want and have sex with another Woman then go home afterwards expecting their Wife to ask no questions whatsoever and to still trust and love him as of nothing had ever taken place or how some Men can be so abusive with their own Wife and yet with other Women never raising a finger but when they get Home all hell breaks lose and some Women put up with that shit and say well he loves me he just had a bad day, but come on Ladies if he has abused you for a day or a month or a year that's to damn long and most Women would say well nobody else would want me, that's just an excuse to stay in the abusive relationship, Women need to ask themselves a question do I love him or do I love myself more, most Women would say I love myself and him equally which is bullshit since any Woman is going to love herself more especially where there is children involved and even if not she will love herself more to put up with his abuse because she will value her life since life is very precious and there is no life worth living through abuse or a cheating spouse even though the marriage vows say through better or worse it does not say any where about abuse or going through life afraid to even breath without fear something might set him off and the abuse would start again, she thinks hey I would rather live alone than to put myself through the pain and humiliation living like this in constant fear of my own life, as she moves into her own Apartment she feels more relaxed and she feels safe she hears a knock at the door one evening and she opens the door without first looking through the peep hole on the door but she manages to close the door however with his pounding on the door she is extremely frightened when a neighbor calls her to ask if she is alright she says well no not really the neighbor says well you should call the police if your scared she said your so right thank you the neighbor says ok take care as she hangs up she calls the police and she tells them that she moved in her Apartment to get away from his abuse and now he found out where she lived and will not leave as the police arrive where they ask what is the problem as he continues pounding on the door the officer goes to subdue the Man noticing that he is drunk calls for backup but as the backup arrives he has the Man in cuffs and in the back seat of his Car as he is telling the Woman that there is nothing to worry about he tells her that if she has anymore problems to just call she says I will officer thank you as she closes the door and the officer drives off to the station where he files driving while intoxicated charges plus resisting arrest and disturbing the peace as the drunk empties his pockets he pulls out a baggy with marijuana in it which added to the charges in possession of illegal substance, then the officer takes him back putting him in a jail cell closing the door, then one day she calls the police station asking to speak to the officer as he answers hello she says her name and where she lives the officer says I can't tell you a lot but you don't need to worry about him anymore she started crying and the officer said what's wrong she said oh nothing officer I am just so relieved knowing that I don't have to worry he said I'm glad we are here to protect and serve call us if you have anymore problems she said thank you officer I will, the Woman felt very comfortable so she even began cleaning her Apartment almost naked wearing just her bra and panties just as she was finishing the cleaning someone knocked she said just a minute as she put on one of her silk night gowns on since she had not unpacked her house coat and had no way of knowing exactly what box it was in and went to answer the door as she opened the door surprised to see a nice looking Man standing there he said hello my name is Fred she said Fred since he was in plain clothes he said I'm the officer that arrested that drunk at your door, she said oh yes come in have a seat let me go get something else on, he said that's ok I just felt like coming over to make sure that you were ok she said yes Fred I'm fine thanks to you he said your welcome he said well I best go she said what's your rush he said I didn't want to interrupt anything you were doing but I just wanted to stop by and check on you and to leave you one of my cards she said thank you very much he said your very welcome she said hey by the way my name is Laura of course what wrong with me I'm sure you knew that already with this address given over the radio, Fred said yes but it is nice to meet you Laura she said it's nice meeting you also Fred, Laura said do you think you Wife would mind if I gave you a kiss Fred said I'm not married and Laura said what a handsome Man like you I bet there Women knocking at your door constantly Fred smiled and said why no I am a loner but with my job I never know when I might be called out or something Laura said I understand being a policeman as Laura walked over to Fred and passionately kissed him.

About the Author

I enjoy writing just to be writing and which might help save a relationship from a divorce since I have been through many experiences myself satisfying the Woman is so very important in any relationship and it has been my experience that if a problem comes up going some where to cool off and then talking about it will do more good than saying things to the Woman that you love and hurting her more besides a Woman is to be loved and not to be used as a human punching bag.